EMMA'S POEM

The Voice of the Statue of Liberty

by Linda Glaser

with paintings by Claire A. Nivola

Houghton Mifflin Harcourt
Boston New York

The text of this book is set in Stempel Garamond.
The illustrations are painted with watercolors and gouache.

The Library of Congress has cataloged the hardcover edition as follows:
Glaser, Linda.
Emma's poem: the voice of the Statue of Liberty/by Linda Glaser; illustrated by Claire A. Nivola.
p. cm.
1. Lazarus, Emma, 1849–1887—Juvenile literature. 2. Statue of Liberty (New York, N.Y.)—Juvenile literature.
3. Poets, American—19th century—Biography—Juvenile literature. 4. Women social reformers—New York
(State)—New York—Biography—Juvenile literature. 5. Jews—New York (State)—New York—Biography—
Juvenile literature. I. Nivola, Claire A., ill. II. Title.
PS2234.G55 2009
811'.4—dc22
2009026924

Acknowledgments

In striving for historical accuracy, I am grateful to Christine Schmid Engels of the American Jewish Archives, and
Jeff Dosik and Denise Foehr of the National Park Service, Statue of Liberty National Museum, for their help. In
addition, I'm grateful to Esther Schor for generously answering my questions and connecting me with Bette Roth
Young. I wish to thank Bette Roth Young for sharing her passion and expertise as she carefully reviewed my manu-
script. She won my heart instantly with her warm welcome into the "Lazerite Sisterhood." I also wish to thank Ann
Rider for loving this story from the beginning and then gently but firmly pushing me further.

For further reading and inspiration I suggest the following:

The World of Emma Lazarus by H. E. Jacob (Schocken Books, 1949)
I Lift My Lamp: Emma Lazarus and the Statue of Liberty by Nancy Smiler Levinson (E. P. Dutton, 1986)
Emma Lazarus by Esther Schor (Schocken Books, 2006)
Emma Lazarus in Her World: Life and Letters by Bette Roth Young (Jewish Publication Society, 1995)

To hear schoolchildren singing "Give Me Your Tired, Your Poor" visit
kids.niehs.nih.gov/lyrics/liberty.htm.

ISBN: 978-0-547-17184-5 hardcover
ISBN: 978-0-544-10508-9 paperback
ISBN: 978-1-328-82635-0 special markets paperback
061718.5K3/B1058/A7

Manufactured in China
SCP 10 9 8 7 6 5 4 3 2 1

4500642350

To the immigrants then and now — L. G.

Jewish Heroes

The Jewish people have many heroes: women and men whose lives have changed the world, who have so strongly affected others that we want to remember and pay tribute to them and, often, emulate their actions. These heroes may be familiar to us through their discoveries, their bravery, their writing, or their talent in some special area – sports, science, or art, for example. Perhaps they lived long ago, or you might have seen them interviewed on television last night! They could have been heroic in childhood or as adults. Judaism might play an obvious role in their lives or it may live quietly in the background of our knowledge of them; however, their "Jewishness" informs who they are, the choices they make, and their legacy.

This book is one in a PJ Library® series about Jewish heroes. Reading about these extraordinary people will give you a window into their fascinating personalities and their memorable lives. We hope you will be so interested that you'll go beyond the pages of this book to learn even more. . . .

Who knows? One day you could be the subject of such a book!

Enjoy your reading!

Harold Grinspoon and Your Friends at PJ Library

When Emma was a little girl,
she had plenty of everything—
plenty of pretty dresses,
plenty of good food,
and plenty of love from her family.

She lived in a large, comfortable house
in New York City
with her mother and father
and her sisters and brother.
She loved to read.
And she had plenty of books.
She loved to write.
And she had plenty of time
to create stories and poems.

All the people Emma knew
had plenty of good food
and fine clothes.
They had plenty of everything.

Even when Emma was all grown up,
and by then a well-known writer,
she still only knew people
who had plenty of everything.

But one day, Emma visited Ward's Island
in New York Harbor.
There she met very poor immigrants
whom she had only heard about.
They had come a long way across
the ocean by boat.

They wore ragged clothing
and looked tired and sad.
Some were sick.
All of them were hungry.
They were the poorest people
Emma had ever seen.
Her heart hurt to see them.

They were Jews like Emma.
Some were well educated like Emma.
But they had been treated very badly
in Eastern Europe.
Their homes had been burned.
Friends and relatives had been killed.

They had made the long, hard journey
to America, hoping for a better life.
Emma felt she must help them.

At that time in the 1880s
people believed that a fine lady like Emma
should not mingle with poor people.
But Emma often visited the immigrants.
She helped them learn English
and get training for jobs.
In time she befriended many of them.

Emma knew that in her own city
many people did not care about the immigrants.
People said they were so ragged and poor,
they'd ruin the country.
In those days, most women kept their thoughts quiet.
But Emma wrote about the immigrants
for the newspaper and in poems.

She told, with great feeling,
how badly they needed help.
She explained that with help
they'd give back to the country.
Many people read her writing.
Some began to care.
But still many did not.

One day, Emma heard about a statue
being constructed in France
as a gift of friendship for the United States.
It was meant to show the great love of liberty
that both countries shared.

The statue was huge—
one hundred fifty-one feet tall!
The arm holding the torch
was forty-two feet long!

The statue would be erected
right in New York Harbor.
But first, money was needed
to build a very large pedestal
for the statue to stand on.

To raise money,
many well-known American writers
such as Mark Twain and Walt Whitman
were asked to write something.
Emma was asked to create a poem.
The whole collection would be sold
to help pay for the statue's pedestal.

Emma Lazarus always wrote
what she cared about.
Now she thought hard.
What did she want to say?

At that time, the Statue of Liberty
had nothing to do with immigrants.
But Emma knew that immigrants
would see the huge woman
when their boats arrived
in New York Harbor.
Wouldn't they wonder
why she was there?
What might they think?
What might they hope?

And what if the statue
were a real live woman?
What might *she* think
when she saw immigrants
arriving hungry and in rags?
What might she feel?
And, Emma pondered,
what would the statue say
if she could actually speak?

Emma took up her pen
and began to write.

Emma's poem was the only one read
at the large celebration in 1883
to raise money for the pedestal.
Those listening heard a powerful new voice
speak up for the immigrants.

In the last few lines of Emma's poem,
they heard the huge statue send out a welcome
to immigrants and boldly tell the world,
Give me your tired, your poor,
your huddled masses yearning to breathe free . . .

Three years later, in 1886,
when enough money had been raised,
the statue was packed into 214 crates,
shipped across the Atlantic Ocean,
and erected in New York Harbor
on top of the pedestal.

Sadly, Emma lived only a short time
after the statue was erected.
Although she knew that her poem
had helped buy the pedestal for it,
and she knew that her poem
gave the huge woman
a strong and caring voice,
she did not know
that in the years to come
her poem would do much more.
Slowly, over time,
Emma's poem stirred the hearts and minds
of people around the nation.

Twenty years after Emma wrote it,
a friend had the poem engraved on a plaque
and placed inside the entrance
to the pedestal of the Statue of Liberty
for all visitors to see.

Thirty years after that, Emma's poem
was printed in school textbooks
and children around the country
learned to recite it.

Then, more than sixty years after Emma wrote her poem,
the last five lines of it,
the statue's bold words, were set to music
by the famous songwriter Irving Berlin
and sung on Broadway.

Soon, schoolchildren around the country were singing,
Give me your tired, your poor,
your huddled masses yearning to breathe free.

Now the huge statue was much more
than a gift of friendship
from France to the United States.

Because of Emma's poem,
the Statue of Liberty
had become the mother of immigrants.
And her torch was a lamp held out to welcome them.

Today, Emma's poem is so well known
that when people look at the Statue of Liberty
they can almost hear her speaking,
Give me your tired, your poor,
Your huddled masses yearning to breathe free,
The wretched refuse of your teeming shore.
Send these, the homeless, tempest-tost to me,
I lift my lamp beside the golden door!

AUTHOR'S NOTE

Emma Lazarus was a writer at heart. Born in 1849 into a wealthy Jewish family in New York City, she wrote many poems, stories, and articles during her short life and was already a highly respected writer at thirty-eight years old when she died of Hodgkin's disease.

Emma was also a fervent humanitarian. Dr. Gottheil of the Hebrew Immigrant Aid Society brought her to Ward's Island because she was already expressing concern for the immigrants.

Witnessing their terrible poverty, Emma became fiercely determined to help. She worked in the Hebrew Immigrant Aid Society and also raised money for it, strongly believing that if immigrants received job training and education they would contribute to society.

Emma Lazarus wrote "The New Colossus," the poem about the Statue of Liberty, in 1883 when she was thirty-four years old. Thanks to Emma's friend Georgina Schuyler, the poem was engraved on a bronze plaque and placed inside an entryway to the statue's pedestal—thus saving it for posterity.

The bold words that Emma gave the statue to speak are the most famous of all her poetry—and are permanently linked with the statue and known throughout the world. Now on display in the Statue of Liberty Museum, the poem is viewed by millions of visitors each year and continues to stir the hearts of people in the United States and give hope to all those around the world "yearning to breathe free."

The New Colossus
by Emma Lazarus

Not like the brazen giant of Greek fame,
With conquering limbs astride from land to land;
Here at our sea-washed, sunset gates shall stand
A mighty woman with a torch, whose flame
Is the imprisoned lightning, and her name
Mother of Exiles. From her beacon-hand
Glows world-wide welcome; her mild eyes command
The air-bridged harbor that twin cities frame.
"Keep, ancient lands, your storied pomp!" cries she
With silent lips. "Give me your tired, your poor,
Your huddled masses yearning to breathe free,
The wretched refuse of your teeming shore.
Send these, the homeless, tempest-tost to me,
I lift my lamp beside the golden door!"